Contents / Revision Checklist (continued)

After revising each section and fully understanding the content required for y
revision complete column. You should revisit each section before your exam

C000039872

Customer Segmentation

It is vital for businesses to understand who their target customers are, as **all groups of customers differ**. Different groups of customers will have different wants, needs and expectations. Businesses must understand these characteristics about their customers in order to meet different wants and needs.

Customers can vary because of:

➔ **Their requirements** – different groups of customers have different requirements of the products and services a business provides. Vegetarian products, for example, are aimed at people who require products that do not contain meat.

➔ **The amount of money they are <u>able</u> to pay** – different groups of customers will have different budgets. Some customers may have more disposable income, this is the amount of money they have to spend after all their financial commitments (such as their bills) have been paid. Young professionals without children, for example, may have more disposable income than people who are supporting a large family or those customers that are not in regular employment.

➔ **The amount of money they are <u>willing</u> to pay** – having money to spend doesn't mean that customers will spend it! Different customer groups will have varying perceptions on what is affordable and what is classed as expensive.

➔ **Quantity of goods they require** – this is the amount of goods customers are likely to buy, and all customer groups will require different amounts. A family with three children under the age of 2, for example, will require more nappies and baby wipes than a family with just one child under 2 years old.

➔ **Quality of goods they require** – people's judgement of what makes a quality item varies. Some customers will demand much higher quality than others, businesses need to know this of their customers.

➔ **Time and location they wish to purchase the goods** – businesses will need to make sure their products and services are available when and where their target customers want them, or face missing out on vital sales. Some customers, for example, may only purchase certain products online. Businesses need to react to this and ensure they are offering products where and when customers want them.

Market Segmentation

Some products are aimed at everyone; toothpaste, for example, is a common product that most people buy. These are said to be aimed at the **mass market**. Often, however, businesses want to target their products or services at certain groups of customers, this process of identifying and grouping target customers is known as **market segmentation**.

Thinking of an orange helps, the whole orange would be the mass market. Within the mass market, or the orange, are segments.

How can markets be segmented?
Markets can be segmented in many ways, and businesses often segment their market based on more than one category. Commonly, markets are segmented by:

➔ **Age** – how old potential customers are. Some businesses choose to target younger/older customers, some choose to target products at a particular customer age bracket, 18-30 holidays, for example.

→ **Gender** – whether potential customers are male or female. Clothing stores group their products by whether they are intended for males or females, for example.

→ **Occupation** – this is the job potential customers do. It could be as specific as a single job, like a nurse, or a group of jobs like healthcare or professional, for example.

→ **Income** – this is the amount of money potential customers earn. Some businesses aim their products at customers with high incomes, luxury car brands for example, whilst some businesses aim their products at those with lower incomes, budget supermarkets for example.

→ **Geography** – this is where potential customers live. Some products are aimed at people within particular regions. Iron Brew™, for example, is mainly aimed at people living in Scotland.

→ **Lifestyle** – the habits potential customers have are considered to be part of their lifestyle. A business that specialises in cruise holidays, for example, will segment their market to include people who enjoy holidays, particularly by boat.

Benefits of Market Segmentation

Before looking at the benefits of market segmentation for businesses, imagine if a business *didn't* segment their market. They wouldn't have a detailed idea of who their potential customer is or what their wants and needs are, meaning they would be less likely to meet these wants and needs.

Segmenting their market means businesses are more focused on smaller groups of potential customers so, rather than aiming their products or services at everyone, they are much more specific about who they are targeting. Businesses that segment their market are more likely to meet their customers' wants and needs, which means their products have more chance of succeeding and more chance of making a profit. Businesses are also more likely to have repeat custom because they are providing something that people want and/or need and will buy again if necessary.

If markets are segmented, it also means that businesses can target their advertising and promotion at specific groups of potential customers. Businesses that are aiming their product at males, for example, could advertise their products in magazines that are also aimed at males. This means their advertising is more likely to reach their potential customer. Businesses that are targeting products at teenagers may choose to advertise through social media because this is a method that this target audience uses regularly and they are more likely to be exposed to these adverts when compared to radio, magazine or TV advertising in the modern world.

Market Research

Market Research is the process of finding out what customers want and what they need. There are many ways market research can be carried out – but anything a business does to find out about their customers' wants, needs and opinions is known as market research. It can also include looking at existing products or services that are on the market.

If businesses do not carry out market research, they risk developing and launching products that customers do not want and/or do not need. Customers do not usually buy products they don't want or need, so there is more risk for the product to fail if research has not been carried out.

There are many famous examples of products that have 'flopped' because businesses have failed to carry out market research. These failures cost businesses time and money, so carrying out research first is vital!

Methods of Market Research

There are two types of market research; **Primary** and **Secondary**.

Primary research is sometimes called **field research**. This is research that the business carries out themselves; the data or information does not already exist. Carrying out a questionnaire, for example, is classed as primary research – the business generates their own questions specific to what they want to find out from their customers, asks people to complete the questionnaire and then collates and analyses the results. In addition to questionnaires, primary research methods that a business could use include:

➡ **Observations** – watching customers in stores, on High Streets or making use of a product.

➡ **Surveys** – tallying responses to 'quick fire' questions.

➡ **Focus groups** – gathering small groups of people together to answer questions or discuss their opinions.

➡ **Consumer trials** – giving customers products to try out and give their opinions on them afterwards.

Secondary research, which is sometimes called **desk research**, is when businesses look at and make use of data or information that already exists. Using a newspaper to research the prices of products from advertisements in the local area, for example, would be classed as secondary research, as the data used already exists. In addition to using newspapers, secondary research methods that a business could use include:

➡ **Internal data** – using data from within the business, such as sales figures from the cash till system.

➡ **Books and magazines** – using published materials to carry out research.

➡ **Competitors' data** – using data from competitors, such as the prices they charge for products.

➡ **Government statistics and other research material** – using official statistics and data that Governments and other organisations have collected.

Research Advantages and Disadvantages

Primary research can be expensive and can also be time consuming; producing, carrying out and analysing a questionnaire is clearly going to take more time to get results than looking in newspapers at existing information. Carrying out primary research, however, does mean that the business has results that are specific to their own needs, as they have tailored the research to find out exactly what they intended. If a business carries out primary research, they can also make changes to their research if they find their results are not going to be beneficial. They could add additional questions to a focus group, for example, or ask customers to expand on their responses – this cannot be done if carrying out secondary research.

Secondary research is cheaper to carry out than primary research and often takes less time. The outcomes of the research may not be specific to the business's needs, however, as the data that exists was not produced exactly to the business's research objectives.

Customer Feedback

Asking customers for their feedback is a vital part of a business's success. This is because the feedback can be used to make improvements to the business, products or services which should give them more chance of making sales. Giving customers a voice also means they feel more valued and means businesses are able to provide improved customer service and could potentially encourage repeat custom.

There are many ways in which a business could ask their customers for their opinions. In the digital era, customer feedback is often provided online. Customers are able to comment on social media pages or profiles and leave reviews on almost all shopping websites. Businesses can also produce online surveys for customers to complete, which makes analysing data easier as the results are collated electronically.

Traditional methods of gathering customer feedback are still common. Customer comment cards, telephone surveys and verbal comments made to staff are quick and easy ways businesses gather their customers' opinions.

Costs

R065 Task 5

Costs are the things businesses need to pay for. There are lots of things businesses need to pay for; some costs are directly related to manufacturing products, like raw materials, and some are more general bills like gas and electricity (utilities).

The costs businesses have to pay can be grouped as **fixed costs** or **variable costs.**

Fixed Costs

R065 Task 5

Fixed costs are the costs businesses have to pay that do not change based on output; which means these costs stay the same no matter how much of a product or service the business makes or provides.

For example, factories often have to pay rent on their premises. This rent costs the same each month no matter how many products a factory produces. Rent, therefore, is considered to be a fixed cost. So, if a factory's rent is £1,000 per month, it will be £1,000 per month if they produce 15,000 products or if they produce nothing at all – the costs does not change based on the factory's output.

In addition to **rent**, other fixed costs can include:

→ Loan repayments

→ Insurance

→ Advertising

→ Salaries

→ Utilities (gas, electricity, water, telephone, Internet)

→ Website maintenance

Tip: Revise the difference between fixed and variable costs and learn some of the main examples off by heart.

Variable Costs

R065 Task 5

Variable costs, on the other hand, do change based on the business's output. Some costs will change depending on how many products or services a business provides. These costs will increase when the business produces more.

For example, a factory that produces wooden furniture will be buying more wood (their raw material) if they produce more furniture. If they produce no furniture, the cost of their raw material would be £0 because they haven't used any! This cost <u>varies</u> depending on the output of the furniture factory, so is classed as a variable cost.

In addition to **raw materials**, variable costs often include:

→ Stock

→ Packaging

Variable costs are usually given per unit. To get a total amount, multiply this by how many units the business makes/sells.

Total Costs

A business's total costs are calculated by:

Fixed Costs + Total Variable Costs

In the case of the furniture factory mentioned earlier, they have the following costs per month:

Fixed Costs
→ Rent: £1,000 per month
→ Insurance: £100 per month
→ Salaries: £1200 per month
→ Electricity: £150 per month
→ Gas: £50 per month

Total Fixed Costs: £2,500 per month

Variable Costs
→ Wood: £12 per product
→ Packaging: £4 per product
→ Screws etc: £2 per product

So, variable costs of **£18 per product**

Variable Costs for 500 products: £9000

Therefore, their **total costs** are:
£2,500 + £9000
= £11,500

The variable costs per product are multiplied by how many products are made.

Revenue

Revenue is the name given to the money a business makes from selling its products or services. It is the total money coming into the business from sales made – **it is not profit**, because the business still needs to deduct its costs from this money.

Revenue is calculated by:

Selling Price x Number of Sales

> You may be asked to calculate figures over a period of time. So, if you are given the figure **per week**, and are asked for a total **per month**, you will need to multiply your answer by 4.

So, in the case of the furniture factory, if it sells its products for £25 each and sells 500 per month, its revenue would be £25 multiplied by 500 giving a total revenue per month of £12,500.

Profit

Profit is the money left over from the revenue a business has made after costs have been deducted (paid). Some businesses calculate their **profit per unit**, which means the profit it makes when it sells just one product. This is calculated by:

Selling Price per Unit – Total Costs per Unit

> If you get a **minus** figure from this calculation, then the business is making a **loss** (not a profit).

Businesses can also calculate their **total profit** for a given number of products. This can be calculated by:

Sales Revenue – Total Costs

> If given a **monthly** figure and asked for a **yearly** total, you'll need to multiply your answer by 12.

Break-even

Break-even is the term given to the level of output (amount of products) where total revenue is equal to total costs. So basically, it is the point at which a business does not make a profit but does not make a loss either. The break-even point is shown as a number of products (units) and, if businesses calculate this number, they will understand the amount of products they need to produce/sell in order to start making a profit – it's a minimum target they will be aiming for - no business wants to make a loss!

When total revenue matches total costs, the business will **break-even**.

| Selling Price: £50.00 Number Sold: 1000 | Total Revenue (money coming in from sales) £50,000 | | Total Costs (Fixed Costs + Variable Costs) £50,000 | Fixed Costs £10,000 Variable Costs: £40 per product |

In the example above, the break-even point for this business would **1000 units**. They need to sell 1000 products in order to break-even and, when they do sell 1000, they won't be making a loss or a profit.

Break-even Formula

The formula used to calculate the break-even point is:

$$\frac{\text{Fixed Costs}}{\text{Selling Price per Unit} - \text{Variable Cost per Unit}}$$

In the previous example, their break-even calculation would look like this:

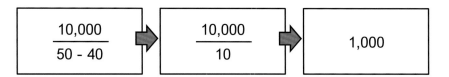

$$\frac{10,000}{50 - 40} \quad \Rightarrow \quad \frac{10,000}{10} \quad \Rightarrow \quad 1,000$$

Break-even Graphs

Break-even can also be worked out and displayed using a graph. The graph has two axes. The y axis is pounds and the x axis is number of products (output).

The graph will have three lines plotted. These are:

→ **Fixed Costs** – this will be a straight line, as fixed costs do not change. Even when no products are made/sold, the fixed costs will still need to be paid.

→ **Total Costs** – this line starts where the fixed costs line does (it can't be lower than fixed costs).

→ **Sales Revenue** – this line always starts at 0 because if you sell no products, you make no revenue.

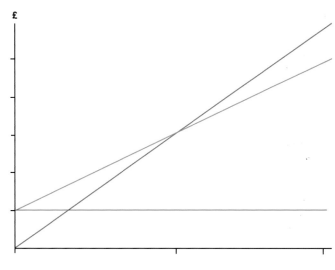

£

Output

Interpreting a Break-even Graph

The point at which the line for total costs and the line for total revenue crosses will be the business's break-even point.

Trace this point down to the output axis (using a dotted line) to highlight the business's break-even point, in this case 1000 units (products).

Luckily, **you won't be asked to draw a break-even graph in your exam** – you will need to understand how to interpret (read) one though and may be asked to identify what the different lines or points on the graph show/represent.

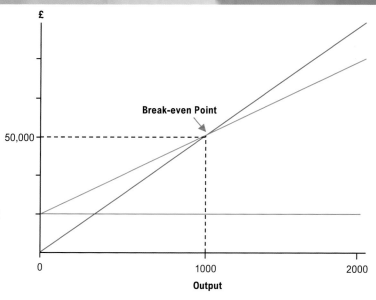

How Break-even is Used

R065 Task 5

As previously mentioned, it is important for businesses to calculate their break-even point. If they don't know what to aim for in terms of unit sales, then they may find out at the end of a trading period (month/year) that they have made a loss. A loss is never a good thing for a business.

Businesses can set sales targets using their knowledge of their break-even point. They can also react and make changes if they think their break-even point is too high. For example, a business could try to cut its fixed costs in order to reduce its break-even point or trial a price change (if their selling price is higher, their break-even point will be lower so they will need to sell less in order to break-even).

The Product Lifecycle

The Product Lifecycle is a theory that suggests that every product has a lifespan, an amount of time that it is manufactured and sold for. For some products, this life is very long. HP™ Brown Sauce, for example, is a product that has been available for more than 100 years and is still very popular today.

On the other hand, the life of some products can be very short. Some products are released and never reach popularity with a customer base. These products are quickly **withdrawn** from the market. The product lifecycle shows sales over a period of time and is split into four different stages.

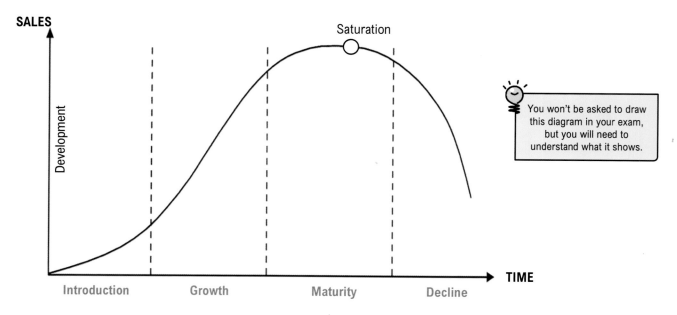

You won't be asked to draw this diagram in your exam, but you will need to understand what it shows.

The Product Lifecycle

The curve on the Product Lifecycle diagram shows the number of sales of a product over a period of time. Each product is individual and will take different amounts of time to pass through each stage.

After the **development** of a product, there are four stages of the Product Lifecyle. These are:

➔ Introduction

➔ Growth

➔ Maturity

➔ Decline

You will need to know the stages of the Product Lifecycle and recognise what is happening to sales of a product during each stage.

Stage	Description	Sales
Development	At this stage, the product is being designed and tested. Businesses will be carrying out their market research to find out potential customers' opinions of the product.	As the product is yet to be released, there are no sales at this stage of the lifecycle.
Introduction	In this stage, the product has just been launched. Customers are buying and trying the product for the first time.	At this stage of the lifecycle, sales are increasing steadily.
Growth	If the product is popular, customers will buy it again (repeat custom). Word is spreading about the product too, so more people are trying it.	Sales rapidly increase due to increased popularity of the product and repeat purchases.
Maturity	At this stage, anyone who wanted to try the product has done so. There are no new customers. Competitors are also releasing similar products onto the market.	Sales at this stage of the lifecycle have **peaked** and, towards the end of this stage, start to reduce.
Decline	At this stage, there are no new customers and repeat custom is also reducing. Businesses must decide whether to **withdraw** the product.	As the name of this stage suggests, sales are declining rapidly.

Within the maturity stage of the Product Lifecycle is a point called **saturation**. This is the point at which sales have peaked, there are no new sales to be made and competitors are releasing similar products, so customers have much more choice and competition is now tough (the market is said to be 'saturated' with increased numbers of similar products/more choice). This is the point at which sales start to reduce.

It is important for businesses to understand which stage of the product lifecycle each of their products is at in order to make the right decisions about their marketing strategies; businesses will ask themselves different questions and make different decisions about their products based on which stage they're at in the lifecycle.

→ Within the **introduction** stage, for example, the business may wish to offer a lower price for their newly launched product, which will later be increased (price penetration), or heavily promote their new product to encourage customers to trial it.

→ Within the **growth** stage, businesses will be looking for ways to **encourage repeat purchases** of their product and trying to get existing customers talking about the product in order to encourage more sales.

→ Within the **maturity** stage, businesses might consider **extension strategies** (see below) to prolong the time the product spends within this stage and prevent the product entering decline; if a business does not identify that their product is in maturity then it may unknowingly enter decline and the use of extension strategies could be delayed or ineffective.

→ Within the **decline** stage, businesses will need to question the viability of their product and consider how long they can continue offering a product with falling sales figures. Ultimately, they will need to ask themselves at what point do they **withdraw** the product from the market.

Extension Strategies

When a product reaches maturity, businesses do not have to just accept that their product will enter decline and eventually be withdrawn, they can decide to do something called an **extension strategy**.

An extension strategy is something a business can do in order to prolong a product's lifecycle and prevent the product from entering the decline stage.

Examples of extension strategies can include:

> You will need to consider which of these strategies would be **appropriate** in different situations; new packaging, for example, may not be effective in extending the life of a mobile phone.

→ **Advertising** – businesses could choose to increase the amount of advertising they are doing for their product, change their adverts so they are more noticeable or change the method of advertising they are currently using (change from radio advertisements to advertising on social media, for example). The aim here is to get people noticing the product exists and encouraging people to try it for the first time or buy it again after perhaps switching to a competitor's product.

→ **Price Changes** – lowering the price of the product could encourage more sales, particularly if the price is lower than that of a competitor.

→ **Adding Value** – businesses could add value to a product by changing its specification. This could be to add additional features to the product, to change the size of the product (50% bigger, for example), to improve the product's quality or to update the product itself ('new improved flavour', for example).

→ **Exploration of new markets** – if products are sold locally (within a single town, for example), businesses could try to expand their customer base by selling regionally (within a county) or even nationally (across the whole country). If a business already offers their products across the whole country, they could try to explore options to sell to Europe or even further afield. With a larger customer base made up of customers who have never bought or tried the product, there is potential for increased sales if the product is popular within these new markets.

→ **New packaging** – businesses could revamp their product's packaging. This gives the product a new lease of a life and makes it stand out to potential customers. It also makes it more noticeable as customers will be used to seeing the old packaging, potentially increasing sales.

Product Differentiation

Product differentiation refers to the ways in which a product stands out from its competitors; something different about a product and potentially the reason a person would buy it over any others. Businesses often capitalise on this difference by using it in their branding, their packaging and their marketing campaigns to encourage customers to trial their product.

Achieving product differentiation is often done through identifying a product's **USP**; its **unique selling point**. This is a feature or added service that is unique about the product when compared to similar products on the market.

Think of any very popular products that are sold worldwide. There must be a reason these products are so successful; what makes them stand out is their USPs. A company selling kitchen roll, for example, might pride itself on planting three trees for every one felled to make their product; this would be their USP and something customers might consider when choosing to buy this product over its competitors'.

Can you think of any other big brands that have unique features in their products, adverts or packaging? **That's likely to be their USP.**

Alongside identifying the unique selling point of a product, businesses can also achieve product differentiation through:

- **Establishing a strong brand image for their goods or services** – if a business builds up a strong brand image then their products can easily be identified. A brand image can be built by creating a logo, strapline and/or distinct product features (like distinct packaging).

- **Getting the balance of product function, cost and appearance correct** – these three key product variables are known as the **'design mix'** and getting this right can improve sales and make products stand out from others. Basically, the product needs to function well, be priced appropriately and have an appearance that is appealing to potential customers.

- **Offering an improved location** – offering improved locations where the product is sold can help the product stand out. If offered on the High Street, for example, a business may choose to also offer the product for sale online through their own website to reach larger markets. The business may also offer the product in more stores across the country or in a different place/store to its competitors.

- **Offering additional features or functions** – products can be made to stand out from others on the market by having additional features or functions added. A new tablet computer could have a small built in projector, for example. This is a rare feature and means the product has been differentiated from others available on the market.

- **Improving the design and appearance of their product** – businesses often make changes to a product's design/appearance so that is stands out against competitors. This can be done during the development stage of the product lifecycle (as part of the 'design mix' discussed above) or during maturity to keep the product up to date and current.

- **Getting their selling price right** – this does not necessarily have to be the cheapest price; some products are priced high to reflect their quality; people often perceive higher priced products to be 'better' than cheaper products . Getting it right is the key; it needs to be what customers are willing to pay. Pricing lower than competitors, however, can help a product differentiate from others that are available on the market.

External Factors on Product Development

An external factor on product development is something outside of the business that will affect their product that they cannot control. These factors can impact on the way the product in manufactured, the quality of the product, the price the product is sold, people's perception of the product or their ability to purchase it.

The 'things' (factors) outside of the business that impact on their products can be broadly grouped into three categories:

→ **Technological Factors** – anything outside of the business relating to technological updates or changes in trends based on technology (the rise in popularity of Internet shopping, for example).

→ **Economic Factors** – anything outside of the business relating to the economy, tax and money; increases in taxes, for example.

→ **Legal Issues** – anything to do with changes in laws or legal requirements for the production and sale of a product within a certain country; product safety standards/laws, for example.

Businesses must be aware of and react to these external factors to ensure their product has the best chance of making sales and to ensure they operate within the law.

Category	Example Scenario	Impact on Product Development
Technological	New machinery has been developed to speed up the production process of a product or improve a product's quality.	Businesses may need to invest in this machinery, costing them money. If they do not invest, then competitors might do so and could be able to manufacture products more quickly or produce a better-quality product than them.
Economic	The country enters **recession** (see below), people are losing their jobs and struggling to manage their finances.	The business is unlikely to invest in developing new products and is more likely to focus solely on surviving.
Legal	A law has been introduced that bans the use of certain materials used within a business's products.	The business will have to source new materials and may need to redesign their product. Their production process may also need changing to meet new legal requirements. All of this will cost money.

The Business Cycle

The Business Cycle is an **economic external factor** and is used to describe the state of a country's economy.

Decline		**Recession**		**Growth**		**Boom**
An economy in decline produces less and sees higher rates on unemployment. *New product development is unlikely.*		A long period of economic decline. Effects include reduced wages and less spending power. *Investment in new product development is highly unlikely.*		An improving economy in which more goods are produced than previous periods. *Businesses are likely to be developing new products.*		If economic growth is *rapid*, this is known as boom. *Businesses may struggle to meet demand for existing products, so are unlikely to work on new developments.*

Considering a Selling Price

R065 Task 5

Price is an important factor when it comes to securing sales of a product and ensuring a product's longevity. Price is often a big influence on whether or not a potential customer actually makes a purchase of a product or either opts for a product sold by a competitor or goes without making a purchase at all.

When deciding on a selling price, businesses must consider:

→ **Income levels of target customers** – when deciding on a selling price, businesses need to consider what their potential customers are able to spend and then what they are willing to spend on the product they are selling. It would be no good for a business to sell a product at a price that the majority of their potential customers could not afford.

→ **Prices of competitors' products** – businesses often look to the prices of similar products on the market when deciding a selling price for their own products. They may choose to set a lower price than that of a competitor in order to stand out to potential customers as a more affordable alternative. They may, however, choose to set a higher price if they wish to stand out as a more quality product or more sought-after brand.

→ **The cost of production** – it is essential for businesses to consider what the product cost them to make when they set their selling price. Businesses often add a percentage on top of their production costs when setting their selling price, this is called their **mark up**. It is very rare for a business to set a price lower than their cost of production for the product they are selling.

Pricing Strategies

R065 Task 5

When setting their prices, businesses can use specific strategies to help them get it right. Each pricing strategy has a different approach to help a business select a selling price for their product. The strategies take into account a range of factors like the demand for the product or the type of product being sold.

A number of pricing strategies have been developed but, for your exam, you need to focus on the four pricing strategies listed below:

→ Competitive Pricing

→ Psychological Pricing

→ Price Skimming

→ Price Penetration

> You need to consider which pricing strategy would be suitable for different situations. A new product to market that has no competition, for example, would not be able to use competitive pricing.

Competitive Pricing

This is when a business looks at what competitors are charging for similar products on the market when deciding on a price to sell their own product for. This strategy is commonly used in crowded markets where there are a lot of products competing for sales, so prices have to be similar or lower than competitors'.

Using the **Competitive Pricing strategy** means that businesses:

✓ Can quickly understand what customers are willing to pay for a product.

✓ Don't have to compete with other businesses based on price; other factors will be taken into account when customers are choosing whether or not to buy the product, like the appearance.

✗ May not be able to cover their production costs for the product if they are basing their selling price on the prices charged by other businesses.

Psychological Pricing

Psychological Pricing is a strategy that is used to give the impression that products are cheaper than they are. Businesses often achieve this by avoiding round numbers for their prices, charging £1.99 for a product rather than £2.00, for example.

Customers aren't stupid, they know this figure is just one penny off £2.00, but when compared with other products and when making a quick decision of which product to buy, this pricing strategy can be very effective.

Using **Psychological Pricing** means that businesses:

- ✓ Could attract customers to buy their product over a competitor's product as it appears cheaper.

- ✓ Have an influence over a potential customers' opinion of how expensive/cheap a product is.

- ✗ Have to be careful not to overuse the strategy; if all their products use this strategy, it may not be effective.

Price Skimming

This pricing strategy involves a business charging a high price for their product when it is first launched and then lowering this price over a period of time. It is a common strategy used when new technology is released; demand is high for the product and there are people who are willing to pay a higher price to be the first to own such products.

Over time, demand reduces as newer products are released and competitors launch similar (cheaper) products. The business reacts by lowering their price.

Using **Price Skimming** means that businesses:

- ✓ Secure sales for a long period of time; firstly, from those willing to pay for the product when released and then from those who want to try the product at its cheaper price.

- ✓ Earn high levels of revenue initially.

- ✗ Risk putting customers off buying/trying the product at the initial high price.

- ✗ Need to ensure their price isn't lowered too late as competitors will quickly release similar products at lower prices.

Price Penetration

Price Penetration is the opposite of price skimming, so businesses charge a lower price initially and then increase this price over time. Unlike price skimming, which was used for a newly released product that has a lot of demand, price penetration is used for new products which are released into a very crowded market and where there are many other similar products.

It is difficult for some newly released products to encourage potential customers to trial them as, for some products, customers get into the habit of buying the same brands over and over again. Breaking brand loyalty is a difficult thing to do, so offering a low price initially is something a business does to encourage customers to do this.

This strategy is commonly used for **consumables**, these are regular purchases that customers make. Think about the brand of coffee, teabags, toothpaste or butter your household buys; is this typically the same or similar brands bought over and over again? A newly released product in these markets needs to have some way of encouraging your household to break those buying habits!

If using **Price Penetration**, a business:

- ✓ Is able to encourage potential customers to trial their product.

- ✓ Is more likely to get a customer to change their buying habits.

- ✗ Loses revenue from the initial low price and potentially could sell for lower than their production costs.

- ✗ Risks putting customers off when the trial price comes to an end.

Advertising Methods

R066 Task 1

Advertising is a way of letting potential customers know about the products and services a business provides. Advertising methods are commonly used to encourage customers to buy a product or service.

Advertising has two purposes; firstly, to **attract** new customers by persuading these potential customers to buy a product or service for the first time. Advertising also has the purpose of **retaining** (keeping) customers; this means to encourage customers to buy the product or service over and over again.

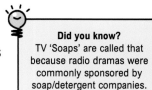

Did you know?
TV 'Soaps' are called that because radio dramas were commonly sponsored by soap/detergent companies.

Methods of advertising commonly used by businesses include:

- ⇒ Leaflets
- ⇒ Social Media
- ⇒ Websites
- ⇒ Newspapers
- ⇒ Magazines
- ⇒ Radio

When deciding on which method of advertising to use, businesses commonly consider:

- ⇒ **Audience** – will the advertising method reach their target customer?

- ⇒ **Budget** – how much the advertising method will cost them, based on numbers it can reach.

- ⇒ **Reach** – how many people will be reached by the advertising method chosen?

Method	Audience	Cost	Reach
Leaflets	Randomly posted or handed out, so there's no specifically targeted audience.	Very cheap to produce; sometimes as little as 2p per leaflet.	Can reach large numbers of people quickly and cheaply. People often throw leaflets away without even looking at them.

Benefits
Drawbacks

Method	Audience	Cost	Reach
Social Media	Adverts can be targeted to specific market segments (genders, ages, interest groups etc.)	Relatively cheap; adverts are charged 'per click'. Social Media accounts are usually free to set up.	Can reach people worldwide. Not everyone uses social media, particularly older audiences.
Websites	Cannot be targeted to specific groups. Audience can access anytime they wish.	Relatively cheap to register a domain and host a website (as low as £10 per year).	Unless promoted on search engines, people have to search for the website or know the web address.
Newspapers	Cannot be targeted at specific groups of people. Usually suited for older target audiences.	Local newspaper adverts are cheaper than national and target people in a specific area/region.	Can reach large numbers of people; though with so much on each page of a newspaper, an advert could be missed easily.
Magazines	As magazines tend to be aimed at people with particular interests or those in particular age brackets, it is easier to target adverts at specific audiences.	Usually expensive, particularly if the magazine is sold nationally.	Can reach large numbers of people depending on the magazine's sales figures. Again, these adverts could easily be missed or ignored.
Radio	Selecting specific radio stations can help target key age groups (Capital FM™ targets younger audiences, for example).	Likely to be the most expensive form of advertising from these options if on a national radio station.	Can reach a large number of people. Possibly more effective/noticeable than newspapers etc. as adverts can include sound effects.

(Circled annotation: Benefits / Drawbacks)

(Box: R066 Task 1)

Sales Promotion Techniques

Businesses can use sales promotion techniques in order to attract new customers to buy their products or services or to retain their existing customers by encouraging repeat purchases.

Similar to advertising methods, businesses consider a range of factors when selecting which sales promotion techniques to use. Cost, target audience and how effective each technique is likely to be will all be considered.

Sales promotion techniques that a business can use include:

⇨ **Discounts** – offering a reduction of the purchase price, usually for a short period of time. This is mostly suited to attracting new customers, though may also encourage a repeat purchase.

⇨ **Competitions** – offering customers the opportunity to participate in competitions to win prizes, some competitions don't require customers to make a purchase of the product and are becoming more popular as part of social media advertising; how often do you see 'like and share to be in with a chance of winning'?

→ **Buy one get one free offers (BOGOF)** – offers like this attract new customers and can encourage repeat purchases. As the name suggests, customers get an identical product for free with their purchase. '3 for 2' is a similar offer that businesses sometimes use.

→ **Point of sale advertising** – point of sale means the point at which a customer buys a product; so point of sale in a physical shop is usually the checkout but can also refer to the display area of the products themselves. Point of sale advertising is, therefore, adverts which are displayed around where customers are shopping or paying for their goods or services.

→ **Free gifts/product trials** – this is when businesses offer free gifts, often with the purchase of their product or service. These added extras can encourage people to choose a product over others that do not offer this.

→ **Loyalty schemes** – loyalty schemes are a sales promotion technique used primarily to retain customers. They offer rewards or discounts if customers purchase a certain number of the product or service. A barber shop, for example, could offer a free 10th haircut after a customer purchases 9 haircuts. Supermarkets (such as Tesco™ ClubCard™) and coffee shop chains also offer such schemes to encourage customers to buy more and continue buying. These schemes suit products or services that people buy regularly but are offered within crowded markets where customers have many options of which products to buy.

Customer Service

Customer service is exactly as the name suggests; it is the way a business and their employees treat a customer before, during and after they make a purchase.

Providing good customer service is something that most businesses strive for; they often include this in their staff training and regularly gather customer feedback to help them improve the level of service they are providing. Good customer service can lead to repeat custom and, conversely, poor customer service can lead to poor reviews, a poor reputation and less repeat custom. A business that has a reputation for poor customer service can also struggle to attract new customers.

A popular saying for businesses is *'if you liked our service, tell your friends or if you think we need to improve, tell us'*. This is because word of mouth and reputation are powerful in attracting new customers.

Businesses can use the following to provide good customer service:

→ **Good product knowledge** – they can demonstrate good knowledge of the products they are selling and pass their advice on to their customers. This can attract new customers, who often have questions about their potential purchase. This can also help retain customers as, once they understand the business and their staff are confident in their knowledge of the products they are selling, they are likely to return should they need similar or replacement products.

→ **Customer Engagement** – a business's employees need to be polite, courteous and professional when dealing with customers in store, over the phone or even during online chats. The employees also need to communicate appropriately with customers. Getting this right could encourage customers to return (retain customers). It can also lead to a positive reputation and therefore could attract new customers too.

→ **After sales service** – people often think that customer service just relates to the time a customer is making their purchase. Whilst that is the time that customer service can be effective in securing a sale, it can also be effective after a sale has been made. Businesses could offer a guarantee on products purchased, free repairs or a free helpline should the customer need further support after their purchase has been made. All of these services can help retain existing customers and can be the reason a new customer might buy a product.

Ownership

There are a range of different types of business ownership. Each type of ownership has different characteristics based on:

→ Number of owners

→ Distribution of profits

→ Decision making

→ Steps required to register/set-up

→ Responsibility for debts (liability; see page 21)

Small businesses usually open as one of the following types of ownership:

→ Sole trader

→ Partnership

→ Limited Liability Partnership (LLP)

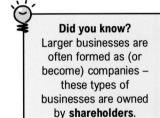

Did you know?
Larger businesses are often formed as (or become) companies – these types of businesses are owned by **shareholders**.

Each type of ownership has its advantages and disadvantages; you will need to be able to explain these advantages and disadvantages for your exam.

Sole traders

A sole trader is a person who sets up and owns their own business. Setting up as a sole trader is relatively easy; an individual just needs to register with HMRC (that's the Government department responsible for collecting taxes in the UK) at some point after opening their business.

Did you know?
Sole traders can still employ workers/staff – but there's only one actual **owner**.

Advantages of sole trader ownership	Disadvantages of sole trader ownership
✓ Easy to set up.	✗ It is difficult for the owner to take time off (for holidays or due to illness).
✓ The owner makes all the decisions.	✗ There is a lot of responsibility for the owner (no shared skills, limited support).
✓ The owner can decide what to do with any profits made.	✗ Unlimited liability (see page 21).

Partnerships

As the name suggests, a partnership is the name given to a business that is owned and operated by two or more people. To set up this type of business, owners must register with HMRC for tax purposes. Each partner pays tax on any profit that has been shared between them from the business.

The way the partnership will operate, the responsibilities of each of the partners and the distribution of profits is usually written out in a document called a 'deed of partnership' before the business is formed.

Advantages of being in a partnership	Disadvantages of being in a partnership
✓ Running of the business is shared, so it is easier to take holidays or time off if ill.	✗ Partners could disagree on business decisions.
✓ Likely to have more capital to set up as funds are coming from more than one person.	✗ Can be complicated for partners to join or leave (may need to be 'bought out').
✓ Owners may bring different skills to the business.	✗ Unlimited liability for all partners (see page 21).

Limited Liability Partnerships

This is a form of partnership in which the owners have **limited liability**, this means that the owners are not responsible for the debts that the business cannot pay. Similar to a traditional partnership, this type of business is owned by two or more people.

To set up a limited liability partnership (LLP), an LLP agreement must be written which states how the LLP will be run. The LLP must also be registered with Companies House and its accounts must be published.

Franchises

Franchising is when a business sells the rights to its name (and the way the business operates) to other people, so they can trade under the same name and format. People buy the rights to a business idea then run their business in the same way as the original/main business runs.

The person opening up a new version of the main business is called a **franchisee**. They own their business but operate it in the same way as the main franchise business. As they own their own business, the franchisee could be a sole trader, partnership, limited liability partnership or a limited company.

Advantages of franchises for the franchisee	Disadvantages of franchises for the franchisee
✓ The business is already established, so less risk compared to setting up with a new idea.	✗ Buying the format will be a higher initial cost than setting up a new idea.
✓ The franchisee will benefit from any advertising the franchisor does.	✗ A percentage of ongoing profits made by the business need to be paid to the franchisor.
✓ The franchisor will give help and support to the franchisee.	✗ Franchisees have less control - changes to the format are not usually permitted.

The owner of the main business that is selling their way of operating is called the **franchisor**.

Advantages of franchises for the franchisor	Disadvantages of franchises for the franchisor
✓ The franchisor's business grows without them having to do very much – the franchisee is opening the business and doing the work.	✗ The business name could get a bad reputation if the franchisee runs their branch of the franchise poorly.
✓ Franchisors are paid for their business idea and continue to get money from an operating franchise's profits.	

Liability

Liability, in business, refers to the responsibility to pay any debts a business may have. There are two types of liability; **unlimited** and **limited**. If owners of a business have **unlimited liability**, then they are responsible for all the debts a business has, even if the business has no more money to pay these debts. If the business cannot pay the debt, the owner or owners must use their own personal money (or even sell their personal possessions) in order to pay back what is owed. Owners of sole trader businesses and ordinary partnerships have unlimited liability; their personal finances and possessions are at risk if the business has debt that it cannot repay from its own funds.

Limited liability, on the other hand, means that owners only stand to lose what they invest in a business. If a business cannot pay its debts, owners who have limited liability are not responsible for repaying this money if the business itself can't. Shareholders, the name given to the people who own shares in companies, and partners in limited liability partnerships (LLPs), all have limited liability.

Sources of Capital

Capital is the money used to start up a business. When people start up a business, the money they use can come from a range of different places (known as sources):

→ Their own savings

→ Their friends and/or family

→ Loans

→ Crowdfunding

→ Small business grants

→ Business angels

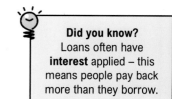

Did you know?
Loans often have **interest** applied – this means people pay back more than they borrow.

Source	Description	Advantages	Disadvantages
Own Savings	This is when the person or people setting up a business invest their own money.	✓ This method will not involve any interest payments. ✓ No application process or requirements to meet.	✗ The amount available is limited to the amount the owner has saved or how much of their money the owner is willing to use.
Friends & Family	This is the when the person or people setting up a business borrow money from their family and/or friends.	✓ There is usually no interest applied to the amount loaned. ✓ No application process or requirements to meet.	✗ Could lead to disagreements and tension if repayment arrangements are not kept.
Loans	This is when the person or people setting up a business borrow money from an institution such as a bank or building society.	✓ Allows people who do not have any savings to raise large sums of money. ✓ Monthly repayments for the same amount make budgeting quite easy.	✗ The owner/s will have to pay back more than they borrow (interest). ✗ Application processes take time, acceptance is not guaranteed.

Source	Description	Advantages	Disadvantages
Crowd Funding	Usually done online, this involves people ('sponsors') giving small amounts of money. The business usually offers something in return for donations (discounts, free trials of the product etc.)	✓ There is no interest payable on this type of capital. ✓ Helps raise awareness of the new business.	✗ Can take a very long time to gather the amount required as people are usually only giving small amounts.
Small Business Grants	This is when the Government, councils or charities offer people money, free equipment or reduced fees (like lower rent or business rates) to get their business started.	✓ The money may not need repaying or, if it does, the interest rate is usually low.	✗ Often, criteria have to be met (e.g. the business may need to be in a poorer area). ✗ Application process can take a long time.
Business Angels	Business Angels are wealthy people who give money to new ventures in return for a stake in the business.	✓ A Business Angel will bring expertise and support to someone starting up. ✓ Suitable for more risky business ideas (that banks may not be confident in).	✗ The business owner/s lose a proportion of their business to the Business Angel.

Business Plans

A business plan is a document drawn up before a business first opens. Business plans are outlines of how a business intends to operate, what the business wants to achieve and how the business will be organised and managed.

Business plans help a new start-up:

→ Make important decisions about their business before they actually get started, helping them avoid time wasting or costly mistakes.

→ Understand whether their plans are viable (likely to succeed/work).

→ Share their ideas with other stakeholders like banks and investors.

> **Did you know?**
> Around 80% of new businesses fail within 18 months of opening.

Business plans are considered to be vital documents for any new start-up. A person who draws up a business plan before opening their business is more likely to succeed because they will have thought of many eventualities before actually opening their business.

Whilst all business plans are different and personal to the new start-up they are written for, they are generally separated into sections titled:

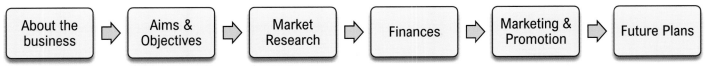

About the business ⇨ Aims & Objectives ⇨ Market Research ⇨ Finances ⇨ Marketing & Promotion ⇨ Future Plans

Within each section of a business plan, the person starting up a new business idea may wish to include:

About the business
→ Who owns the business?
→ Who runs the business on a daily basis?
→ Basic details about the business (What they sell? What times they open? Where they're located? etc.)
→ What will happen to any profits made?
→ Suppliers
→ Employees and their roles

Aims and Objectives
→ The business's aims (what they want to achieve)
→ The business's objectives (how they will achieve their aims)
→ These are sometimes broken down into short and long term aims (after 1 year and after 5 years)

Market Research
→ Details of any market research done before the business starts (see page 4)
→ Outcomes of this research

Finances
→ Sources of capital; where is the money coming from to start the business? (see page 21)
→ Initial expenses (where will the capital be spent?)
→ Cashflow (money coming in to and out of the business)
→ Break-even (see page 8)

Marketing & Promotion
→ Plans for marketing and promotion (see page 16)

Future Plans
→ Future plans for expansion

Functional Areas
Functional Areas are **departments** within a business that carry out specific tasks. These tasks are known as functional activities and can include:

→ Ordering supplies

→ Managing finances

→ Managing the business's employees

→ Producing the products

→ Looking after customers

→ IT Support

In a large business, there will be many different functional areas in which employees have dedicated roles associated to the tasks shown above. In a smaller business however, these tasks are likely to be carried out by a small number of people. In a sole trader business, these functional activities could even all be carried out by the same person.

Departments, or functional areas, of a business have specific names depending on the role they play in the running of the business. Whilst there are many different functional areas, the main ones (and the ones required for your exam) are:

→ **Human Resources** – responsible for managing the employees who work for the business.

→ **Marketing** – responsible for identifying the wants/needs of customers and ensuring these are met.

→ **Operations** – actually producing or selling the goods/services that the business provides.

→ **Finance** – managing the money within the business and reporting on the business's performance.

Human Resources

As the name suggests, this department deals with the people (humans!) employed by the business.

Some of the main duties carried out by this department are:

→ **Recruitment and selection of employees** – this involves identifying whether additional employees are required, advertising posts, interviewing candidates and selecting the right people for each job role.

→ **Training employees** – this involves ensuring all new employees know how to do their job. It also involves ensuring existing employees continue to train and develop in their role.

→ **Performance management** – this involves giving existing employees targets and monitoring if they're met. If not met, this functional area will provide support to the employee to make improvements.

→ **Health and Safety** – this involves ensuring all employees understand the rules of the workplace in terms of health and safety. It also involves ensuring the workplace is a safe environment.

→ **Meeting employment laws** – this department strives to ensure the business operates within the law in terms of employment standards (working hours, holiday pay, sick pay etc.).

Marketing

This functional area focuses on the 4 P's of Marketing (known as the **Marketing Mix**). These are:

→ **Product** – the actual goods/services being sold by the business.

→ **Price** – ensuring customers are willing to pay the price goods/services are being sold for.

→ **Place** – ensuring the goods/services are sold in the correct place.

→ **Promotion** – ensuring the goods/services are advertised and promoted in the correct way.

In order to find out potential customers' opinions of the 4 P's and to find out about products that are already on the market, this functional area regularly carries out **Market Research**.

This functional area also prepares all of the marketing and promotional material the business uses; adverts, for example, will be developed by this functional area.

Operations

In a business that actually produces its own products, this functional area is responsible for the production of these goods.

This functional area:

→ **Plans the production of products** by sourcing raw materials and planning the production process to ensure it is as efficient as possible.

→ **Produces the products** the business sells (makes the products).

→ **Monitors the quality of the products** being produced and investigates ways that quality can be improved.

→ **Manages levels of stock** by ensuring the business does not run out of raw materials or that raw materials do not get damaged or go off whilst in storage.

→ **Focuses on the logistics of the products**. This means that the products are delivered to where they are needed on time or stored appropriately until required.

Finance

The finance function deals with all the money within the business. They monitor **cashflow** (the money coming into and out of the business). They also produce financial reports to monitor the financial performance of the business and to meet the legal requirements of the type of ownership that the organisation operates as (businesses will have to report their earnings to HMRC, for example, in order for tax payments to be calculated).

The finance function also set and monitor **budgets** for the other functional areas; these set out how much money each department has to spend. Setting budgets means the business keeps better control of its spending, particularly if the business is large and has many different functional areas. It also helps ensure the business makes a profit.

Communicating

As mentioned earlier, in smaller businesses some or all of these functional activities will be carried out by one or two people. In larger businesses, however, these functional activities are usually carried out separately by dedicated departments. When this is the case, it is important for each functional area to communicate with one another.

For example, the operations department are responsible for sourcing the raw materials required for the products to be manufactured. If they do not communicate with the finance department, they won't know how much can be spent on raw materials and will struggle to monitor whether the products they are making are actually making any profit. In additional, they will need to communicate with the marketing department to ensure the products they are producing are actually what their customers want and need.

Similarly, all functional areas will need to communicate with the human resources function when they wish to recruit new employees. Human Resources will also communicate with regards to health and safety, particularly with the operations function.

It is now time to fully update your revision checklist on pages 1 and 2 of this booklet.
When you have sat your exam, and no longer need this booklet, is there anyone you could donate it to?